Funny Phonics & Silly Spellings

Louis Fidge

In a hidden cave, far away in a magical land, lives a wise wizard, called Whimstaff. Every now and again, he searches for a young apprentice, so he can pass on his magical English powers. And this time, Whimstaff has chosen you!

Whimstaff shares the cave with a goblin and a little red dragon. Pointy, the goblin, is very clever. The dragon, called Miss Snufflebeam, breathes small puffs of fire. She is clumsy and often loses the wizard's magical letters and numbers.

Pointy has two greedy pet frogs, called Mugly and Bugly, who are very lazy and spend most of their time croaking, eating and sleeping. But every so often, they amaze Pointy by helping with an exercise!

Wizard Whimstaff and his friends are very happy in their cave, solving English problems. Join them on a magical quest to become a fully qualified English wizard!

⭐ Contents

Weird Word Beginnings

I am Wizard Whimstaff and I am here to help you to become a qualified English wizard! You must always look carefully at the beginnings of words. One letter can make all the difference!

I will do a <u>tr</u>ick with a <u>br</u>ick!

Task 1 Try out your magic and make some words, my apprentice!

a br + ick = <u>brick</u>

br + ing = _bring_

br + ag = _brag_

b dr + ag = _drag_

dr + op = _drop_

dr + ip = _drip_

c pr + am = _pram_

pr + od = _prod_

pr + op = _prop_

d cr + ack = _crack_

cr + ust = _crust_

cr + op = _crop_

e gr + ab = _grab_

gr + ip = _grip_

gr + uff = _gruff_

f tr + ap = _trap_

tr + uck = _truck_

tr + ip = _trip_

2

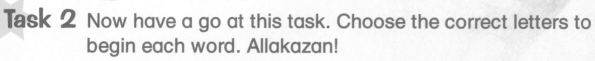

Task 2 Now have a go at this task. Choose the correct letters to begin each word. Allakazan!

a | fr | dr |
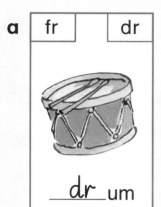
___dr___ um

b | gr | pr |
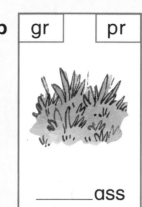
_____ass

c | tr | pr |

_____am

d | tr | br |

_____uck

Task 3 Hey presto! Choose one of the words from Task 2 above to complete each sentence.

a You drive a _____.

b A baby goes in a _____.

c You bang a _____.

d A cow eats _____.

Sorcerer's Skill Check

Do not worry if this seems hard at first. Have a go and see how you get on. Use these beginnings and endings to make some words of your own.

Beginnings
- br
- cr
- dr
- gr

Endings
- ick
- uff
- od
- ag

Some words I can make

brick   brag

_____   _____

_____   _____

_____   _____

You are clever! Award yourself a gold star
and stick it on your certificate on page 32!

Wonderful st Words

I am Pointy the goblin. As Wizard Whimstaff's assistant, I know lots of clever things! Did you know, for example, that the letters st can come at the beginning or at the end of words? You will soon get the hang of them!

I stir the mixture and cast a spell!

Task 1 Now have a try. Write the words you make. Super!

a   _stick_

b   _____

c   _____

d   _____

e   _____

Task 2 A good wizard has to be able to work out riddles. Use the words you made in Task 1 above to help you answer these clues.

a You put this on a letter.

b A bee does this.

c This is made of wood.

d To put boxes on top of each other.

e To stand still.

s	t	a	m	p
s	t			
s	t			
s	t			
s	t			

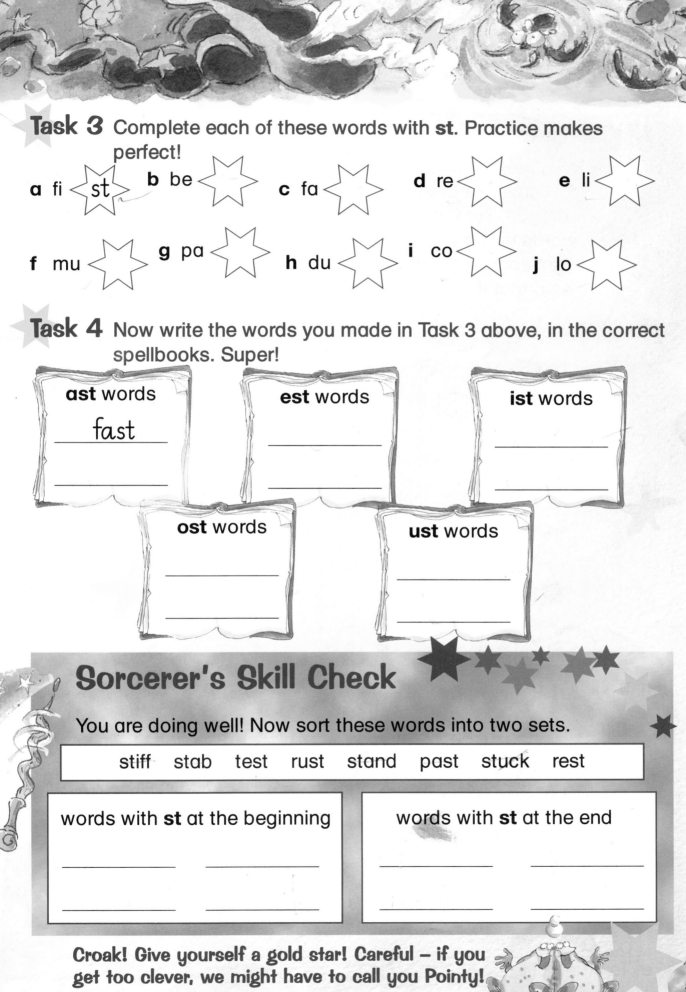

Task 3 Complete each of these words with **st**. Practice makes perfect!

a fi ⟨st⟩   **b** be ✦   **c** fa ✦   **d** re ✦   **e** li ✦

f mu ✦   **g** pa ✦   **h** du ✦   **i** co ✦   **j** lo ✦

Task 4 Now write the words you made in Task 3 above, in the correct spellbooks. Super!

ast words

fast

_____

_____

est words

_____

_____

ist words

_____

_____

ost words

_____

_____

ust words

_____

_____

Sorcerer's Skill Check

You are doing well! Now sort these words into two sets.

| stiff | stab | test | rust | stand | past | stuck | rest |

words with **st** at the beginning

_____   _____

_____   _____

words with **st** at the end

_____   _____

_____   _____

Croak! Give yourself a gold star! Careful – if you get too clever, we might have to call you Pointy!

5

Enchanted ee and oo

I am Miss Snufflebeam, the forgetful dragon. I am supposed to tell you about words that contain ee and oo – but I often get confused! I think Wizard Whimstaff said that if you think of birds and cows it will help!

tweet!

moo!

Task 1 I have asked some friends to help you make some words. Write the whole words you make below.

a p_ee_l **b** f___l **c** h___l **d** p___p **e** k___p **f** d___p

peel _____ _____ _____ _____ _____

g p_oo_l **h** c___l **i** f___l **j** b___t **k** r___t **l** h___t

pool _____ _____ _____ _____ _____

Task 2 Now help me join the pairs of words that rhyme. Write the words here.

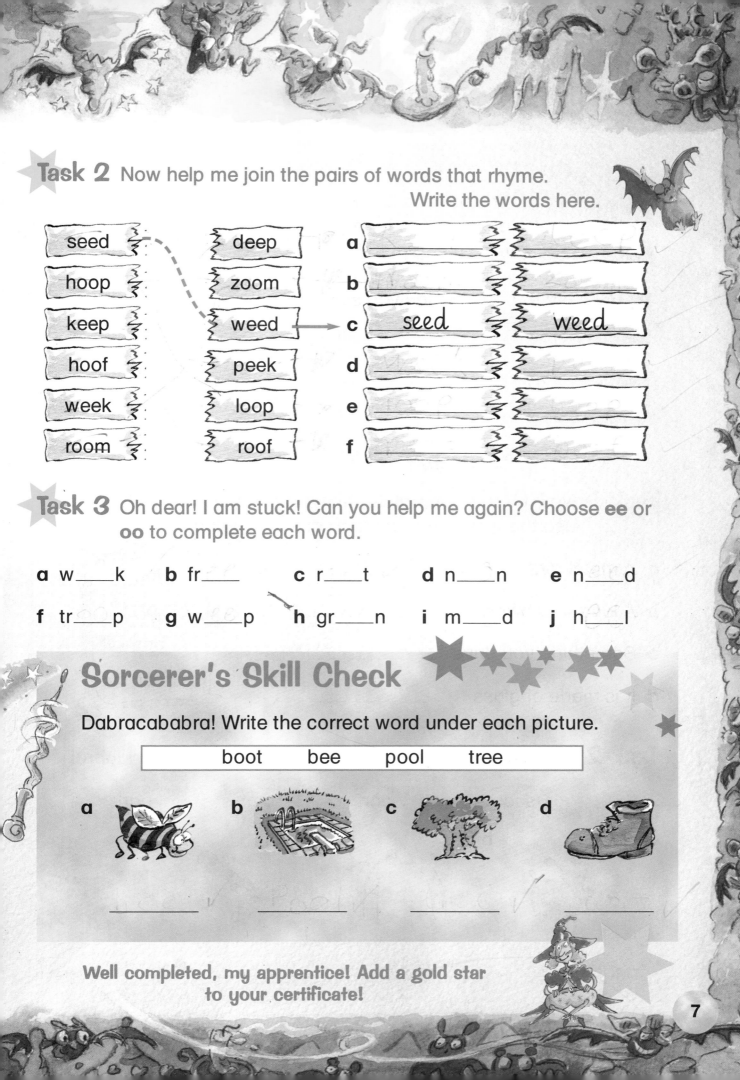

seed	deep	**a**	
hoop	zoom	**b**	
keep	weed →	**c**	seed weed
hoof	peek	**d**	
week	loop	**e**	
room	roof	**f**	

Task 3 Oh dear! I am stuck! Can you help me again? Choose **ee** or **oo** to complete each word.

a w___k   **b** fr___   **c** r___t   **d** n___n   **e** n___d

f tr___p   **g** w___p   **h** gr___n   **i** m___d   **j** h___l

Sorcerer's Skill Check

Dabracababra! Write the correct word under each picture.

boot	bee	pool	tree

a   **b**   **c**   **d**

_____   _____   _____   _____

Well completed, my apprentice! Add a gold star to your certificate!

Astonishing ar

You have to learn to be observant to be a good speller, my apprentice. These two words contain the same letter pattern. Can you spot it?

jar

star

Task 1 Now try this. Complete the words in the mirror with **ar** and use the words you make to answer the riddles.

a A metal rod ___bar___

b A long way away _____

c Something you drive _____

d It is made of glass _____

far

jar

bar

car

Task 2 Write the correct word under each picture. Abracadabra!

| sharp | scarf | arch | bark |

a

b

c

d

____bark____ _____ _____ _____

Task 3 Do the best you can with these word sums. Write the words you make.

a b + ark = ___bark___ **d** p + art = _____

b d + ark = _____ **e** st + art = _____

c sh + ark = _____ **f** ch + art = _____

Task 4 Allakazan! Join the pairs of rhyming words.
Write the words here.

car — spark

march — darn

barn — far

lark — starch

a _____ _____

b _____ _____

c ___car.___ ___far___

d _____ _____

Sorcerer's Skill Check

Hey presto! Complete each word with **ar**.
Write the words you make in the chart.

h_ar_d   f____m   d____t   m____ch   ch____m

p____t   m____k   st____ch   c____d   b____k

arch words	**ard** words	**ark** words	**arm** words	**art** words

**Brain cell alert! You can now add a gold star
to your certificate. Slurp!**

9

Amazing ay and ai

We are Mugly and Bugly, two lazy frogs, and this is a brain cell alert! The letters ay and ai often sound the same when they come together in words.

tr**ay**

The letters ay often come at the end of a word.

r**ai**nbow

The letters ai often come inside a word.

Task 1 Croak! Work out the **ay** words.

a b _ay_   **b** p _a y_   **c** h _ y_   **d** s _ g_   **e** d _ y_   **f** m_____

bay   _Pay_   _hay_   _say_   _day_   _may_

Task 2 Grub's up! Use these **ay** words to answer the riddles.

play –	hay –	tray –	clay	stay	day –

a You carry things on me. _tray_   **d** You make pots with me. _clay_

b Horses eat me. _hay_   **e** You do this for fun. _play_

c The opposite of night. _day_   **f** The opposite of go. _stay_

Task 3 Write the words under the correct pictures. Is it time for a snooze yet?

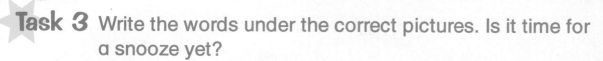

| pail | paint | afraid | train |

a _____ **b** _____ **c** _____ **d** _____

Task 4 Slurp! Help us make these words.

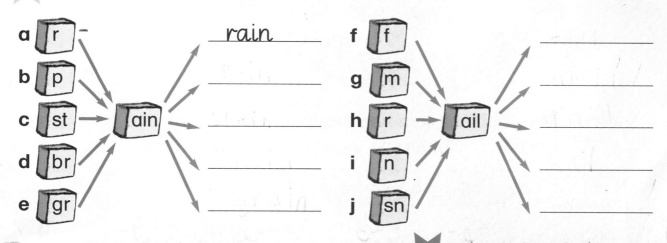

a r → _rain_

b p

c st → ain

d br

e gr

f f

g m

h r → ail

i n

j sn

Sorcerer's Skill Check

Find and circle the hidden **ay** and **ai** words for us.
We are too tired to do it!

a w r t (s w a y) d h y

b z x c v b w a i t n

c m n f a i n t j k l

d q d i s m a y p g f

e y t r w d s p r a y

f c h a i n z x c v b

Excellent work!
Award yourself a gold star. Super!

11

Obliging oi and oy

A good speller has to listen carefully to sounds in words, my apprentice. The letters oi and oy make the same sound in words.

bòil

annoy

The oi usually comes inside a word

The oy usually comes at the end of a word.

Task 1 Miss Snufflebeam has dropped these words and got them all mixed up. Colour the **oy** words **red**. Colour the **oi** words **blue**.

a boy   b boil   c coin   d joy   e toy   f hoist

g enjoy   h choice   i annoy   j noise   k destroy   l foil

Task 2 Now write the words in the correct books for her. Abracadabra!

oy words		oi words	
Joy	annoy	noise	foil
toy	enjoy	coin	hoist
boy	destroy	boil	choice

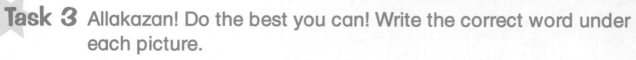

Task 3 Allakazan! Do the best you can! Write the correct word under each picture.

coin	toy	point	destroy

a

b

c

d

_____   _____   _____   _____

Task 4 Now have a go at this. Use the best word to fill in the spaces.

point	enjoy	joy	boil	toy	voice	boy

a I __ __ __ __ __ doing magic tricks.

b You can __ __ __ __ eggs in water.

c The arrow had a sharp __ __ __ __ __ .

Sorcerer's Skill Check

Don't worry if this seems hard at first. Complete each word with either **oi** or **oy**.

a sp __ __ l **d** m __ __ st **g** j __ __ **j** t __ __

b n __ __ sy **e** empl __ __ **h** ann __ __ **k** j __ __ nt

c ch __ __ ce **f** destr __ __ **i** b __ __ **l** av __ __ d

Oh dear! Have you finished already?
You must have worked hard! Have a gold star.

Apprentice Wizard Challenge 1

⭐ **Challenge 1** Make these words.

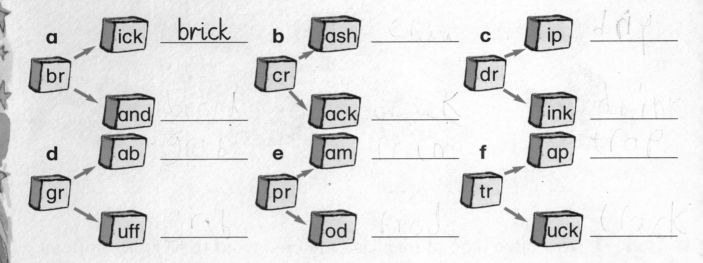

a br → ick _brick_   br → and _____

b cr → ash _____   cr → ack _____

c dr → ip _____   dr → ink _____

d gr → ab _____   gr → uff _____

e pr → am _____   pr → od _____

f tr → ap _____   tr → uck _____

⭐ **Challenge 2** Read the story. Underline the words which end with **st**.

> One day my friend and I had a race. It was cold. There
>
> was some frost on the grass. The race had just begun when
>
> Sam fell and hurt her wrist. Then a mist came down so Ben
>
> sat and had a rest. Ben lost. He came last. I ran fast. You
>
> could not see me for dust! I won. I was the best!

⭐ **Challenge 3** Read the riddles. Complete each word with **ee** or **oo**.

a You eat it.   f_o_ _o_d

b It is on a house.   r_o_ _o_f

c It comes after two.   thr_ _ _

d You swim in this.   p_ _ _l

e Seven days in it.   w_ _ _k

f It is part of a foot.   h_ _ _l

g You see this at night.   m_ _ _n

h An insect that buzzes.   b_ _ _

14

Challenge 4 Match the beginnings and endings of these words.

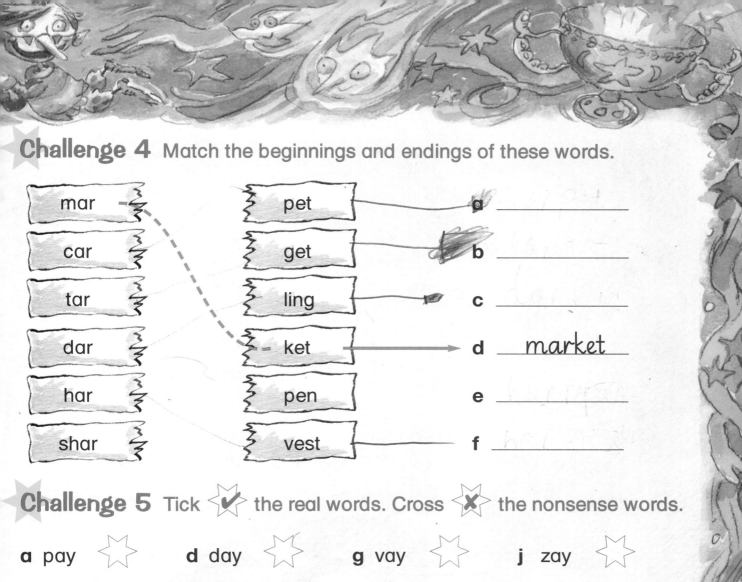

mar		pet		a _____
car		get		b _____
tar		ling		c _____
dar		ket		d _market_
har		pen		e _____
shar		vest		f _____

Challenge 5 Tick ✔ the real words. Cross ✘ the nonsense words.

a pay ☆   **d** day ☆   **g** vay ☆   **j** zay ☆

b blay ☆   **e** clay ☆   **h** way ☆   **k** glay ☆

c play ☆   **f** tray ☆   **i** kray ☆   **l** sway ☆

Challenge 6 Choose **oi** or **oy** to complete the words.

a b ___ ___   **d** j ___ ___   **g** v ___ ___ ce   **j** p___ ___ nt

b t ___ ___   **e** empl ___ ___   **h** ch ___ ___ ce   **k** conv ___ ___

c t ___ ___ let   **f** destr ___ ___   **i** p ___ ___ son   **l** ann ___ ___

You have worked hard, my apprentice!
You deserve a gold star for your effort.

Incredible igh

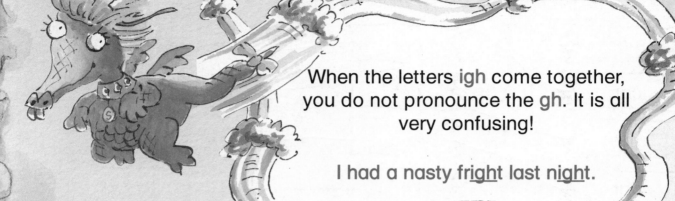

When the letters **igh** come together, you do not pronounce the **gh**. It is all very confusing!

I had a nasty fr<u>igh</u>t last n<u>igh</u>t.

Task 1 Oh no! I think I need some help with these! Help me make some **igh** words and then write the whole words below.

a h<u>igh</u>   **b** s___   **c** n___   **d** th___   **e** r___t   **f** s___t

<u>high</u>

Task 2 My head hurts! Help me write an **igh** word that means the opposite of:

a low   **b** left   **c** dim   **d** loose   **e** blindness **f** day

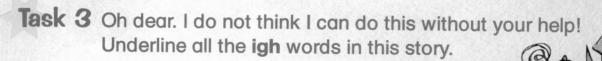

Task 3 Oh dear. I do not think I can do this without your help! Underline all the **igh** words in this story.

The princess gave a deep sigh. She had been locked up in a high tower by a wicked queen. She was frightened. There was not much light at night. Just then there was a sound right outside. The princess looked out. What a sight met her eyes! A handsome prince was there on a white horse. He threw up a rope with all his might. The princess held on tight as she climbed down. She was free at last.

Task 4 Rabracadada! Now make a list of the **igh** words you found in the story.

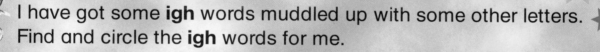

_____ _____ _____ _____ _____

_____ _____ _____ _____

Sorcerer's Skill Check

I have got some **igh** words muddled up with some other letters. Find and circle the **igh** words for me.

a a b c d h m i g h t f g j

d g f n i g h t x w y t g q p

b d b r i g h t a q m x n d

e n m s i g h n t y z x w

c s f r i g h t q w e r t y u

f d x v b c z h i g h x r l

Good work! You have earned yourself a gold star!

Fantastic y

Have you noticed that many words end in y? You have to be careful how you say them, because the y can have two different sounds.

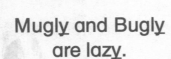

Mugly and Bugly are lazy.

The y in some words sounds like ee.

Miss Snufflebeam can fly.

The y in some words sounds like ie.

Task 1 Practice makes perfect! Add **y** to complete each word and then write the new word.

a baby _baby_

b m____ _____

c tin____ _____

d fl____ _____

e b____ _____

f bod____ _____

g tr____ _____

h hand____ _____

i lad____ _____

j cr____ _____

k cop____ _____

l wh____ _____

Task 2 You will have to listen carefully now. Say the words you made in Task 1 above. Write the **y** words that sound like **ee** in the bee's box. Write the **y** words that sound like **ie** in the fly's box.

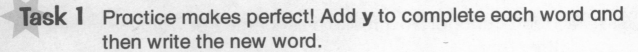

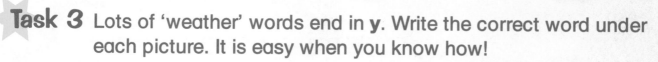

Task 3 Lots of 'weather' words end in **y**. Write the correct word under each picture. It is easy when you know how!

foggy	sunny	rainy	snowy

a

b

c

d

_____   _____   _____   _____

Task 4 Match the words with their meanings. Super!

dry	funny	penny	reply	supply	poppy

a To answer _____

b To provide _____

c A flower _____

d The opposite of wet _____

e A coin _____

f Amusing _____

Sorcerer's Skill Check

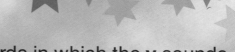

Have a try at this. Colour red the words in which the **y** sounds like **ee**. Colour blue the words in which the **y** sounds like **ie**.

lumpy   fry   multiply   happy   tiny

risky   empty   apply   rely   shy

Croak! Get yourself a gold star. We are going to get ourselves something to eat!

19

Introducing the Magic e

Watch carefully, my apprentice! I want to show you a magic spelling trick. Notice that when I add a **magic e** to the **end** of some short words, it makes the sound of the **vowel** in the **middle** of the word **say its name**!

Allakazan! Change a <u>cap</u> to a <u>cape</u> for me! Add a <u>magic e</u> and you will see!

Task 1 Now try it yourself! Add a **magic e** to each word. Write the new words you make. Hey presto!

a hat + e   = <u>hate</u>   **e** mad + e   = _____

b can + e   = _____   **f** rid + e   = _____

c pip + e   = _____   **g** win + e   = _____

d rob + e   = _____   **h** cut + e   = _____

Task 2 Now make the **magic e** vanish! Write the word you are left with each time. Do not worry if it seems hard at first!

a tape   = <u>tap</u>   **e** mate   = _____

b cape   = _____   **f** hide   = _____

c pine   = _____   **g** shine   = _____

d rode   = _____   **h** mope   = _____

Task 3 Choose the correct word for each picture. Abracadabra!

a | hat | hate | **b** | rid | ride | **c** | mop | mope | **d** | tub | tube |

_____hat_____   _____   _____   _____

Task 4 Miss Snufflebeam has made a mistake in each sentence. Write each sentence again. Correct the underlined word.

a I <u>cane</u> ride my bike.

_____I can ride my bike._____

b I drink water from the <u>tape</u>.

_____

c I can <u>wine</u> the race.

_____

d I <u>hop</u> you get well soon.

_____

Sorcerer's Skill Check

I have hidden some **magic e** words. Find and circle them to make them appear!

a a b c d ⟨m i l e⟩ f g j   **d** n m h o p e n t y z x w

b g f d p a n e y t y u p   **e** s h i n e q w e r t y u k

c d c u b e z a q m x n d   **f** d x v b c z b a r e x r l

Dabracadada! You have won another gold star!
Well done!

Advanced Magic with e

Brain cell alert! When you
see a magic e at the end of a word,
remember that it makes the vowel in the
middle of the word say its name! Croak!

sn<u>a</u>ke   sh<u>i</u>ne   b<u>o</u>ne   t<u>u</u>be

Task 1 Try out some magic tricks and make some new words using
ake. Write the whole new words you make below.

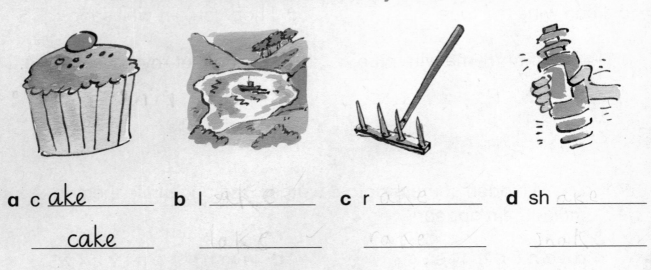

a c <u>ake</u>   **b** l <u>ake</u>   **c** r <u>ake</u>   **d** sh <u>ake</u>

<u>cake</u>   <u>lake</u>   <u>rake</u>   <u>shake</u>

Task 2 Croak! Now try and make some new words with **ame.**
Write the whole new words you make below.

a c _____   **b** s _____   **c** bl _____   **d** sh <u>ame</u>

_____   _____   _____   <u>shame</u>

Task 3 Grub's up! Join up the rhyming words. Write the words here.

side	smile	a _____ _____
pile	rise	b _____ _____
hive	wide	c *side* *wide*
wise	five	d _____ _____

Task 4 Sort out these rhyming words while we have a drink! Slurp!

like   hike   file   wide   nine   mile
fine   side   shine   smile   bike   hide

a Words that rhyme with **glide**:
_____ _____

b Words that rhyme with **pile**:
_____ _____

c Words that rhyme with **pike**:
_____ _____

d Words that rhyme with **pine**:
_____ _____

Sorcerer's Skill Check

Thank goodness! It is the last activity. Now we can have a snooze! Match the correct word to its meaning.

mule   prune   tube   tune

a Something you hum ____*tune*____

b A dried plum ____*prune*____

c A hollow pipe ____*tube*____

d Like a donkey ____*mule*____

Well tried. Your spelling is improving! Have a gold star.

Using ou and oa

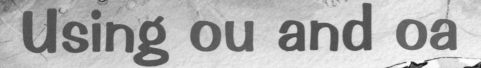

Here is a fact to help you with your spelling!
The patterns oa and ou never come at the end of a word.

A toad croaks. A mouse makes a squeaking sound.

Task 1 Find the rhyming pairs of words in the cloak. You will soon get the hang of it!

boat   soak   coast
toad   toast   coat
moan   road   cloak   groan

Write the words here.

boat	coat
_____	_road_
_____	_coat_
_____	_groan_
_____	_soak_

Task 2 Look carefully. Find and circle the words with the same letter pattern in each line. Super!

a shout   loud   house   hound   about

b proud   couch   cloud   mouth   count

c pound   sound   south   spout   house

d count   scout   crouch   amount   proud

Task 3 It is easy when you know how! Complete each word with
either **oa** or **ou**.

a   b   c   d

t __ __ d   cl __ __ d   m __ __ se   m __ __ th

__toad__   _____   _____   _____

Task 4 I have made some pictures and letters disappear! Complete
each word with **oa** or **ou** and draw the missing pictures.
Super!

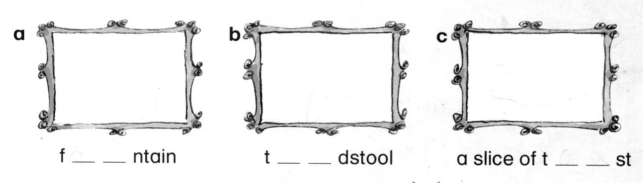

a   b   c

f __ __ ntain   t __ __ dstool   a slice of t __ __ st

Sorcerer's Skill Check

It is time to try out your magic now. Write some **ou** words and
some **oa** words below.

ou words	**oa** words
_____ _____	_____ _____
_____ _____	_____ _____

Slurp! Give yourself a gold star!
We are going to give ourselves a snack!

Wacky wh and ph

Two common letter patterns you need to know are **wh** and **ph**.

a <u>wh</u>istling ele<u>ph</u>ant

You put your lips together when you whistle.

The **ph** makes a **ff** sound in words.

⭐ **Task 1** Now try making some **wh** and **ph** words. Do not worry if it seems hard at first. Allakazan!

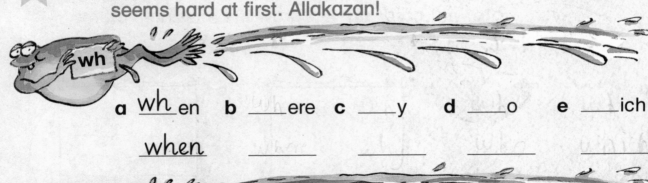

a <u>wh</u>en **b** <u>wh</u>ere **c** ___y **d** ___o **e** ___ich

<u>when</u> _____ _____ _____ _____

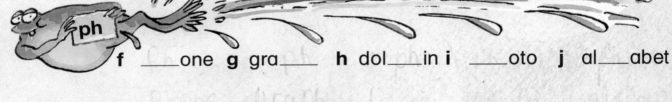

f ___one **g** gra___ **h** dol___in **i** ___oto **j** al___abet

_____ _____ _____ _____ _____

⭐ **Task 2** Look carefully at the words you made, young apprentice.

Write a **wh** word with:

a three letters ___ ___ ___   **b** four letters ___ ___ ___ ___

Write a **ph** word with:

c five letters ___ ___ ___ ___ ___   **d** seven letters ___ ___ ___ ___ ___ ___ ___

26

Task 3 I have made some letters from these words vanish. Choose **wh** or **ph** to complete each word.

a _w_ _h_ iskers **b** tele __ __ one **c** __ __ ale **d** __ __ eel

e ele__ __ ant **f** dol __ __ in **g** __ __ eat **h** al __ __ abet

Task 4 Hey presto! Choose a word from Task 3 above to go under each picture.

a    **b**    **c**    **d**

_____   _____   _____   _____

Sorcerer's Skill Check

Find and circle five **wh** words and five **ph** words in the puzzle.

Write them here.

a	b	w	h	e	e	l	c	d	f
g	h	j	k	l	p	h	o	n	e
w	h	i	t	e	m	p	o	q	r
s	t	e	l	e	p	h	a	n	t
u	v	x	w	h	i	s	k	z	a
d	o	l	p	h	i	n	b	c	d
e	w	h	i	s	p	e	r	f	g
h	i	n	e	p	h	e	w	j	k
l	m	o	p	q	w	h	e	a	t
a	l	p	h	a	b	e	t	r	s

wheel   _____

_____   _____

_____   _____

_____   _____

_____   _____

You have done a super job! Add a gold star to your certificate.

Apprentice Wizard Challenge 2

Challenge 1 Underline the 'hidden' **igh** words. Write each word you find.

a qwe<u>high</u>rty _____

b dfgthighjk _____

c tightmnbvc _____

d zxcmightvb _____

e xlightaqwr _____

f uiopsighas _____

g bsightbnmv _____

h arightdfgh _____

i nmfightkjh _____

j asdfgbright _____

Challenge 2 Sort the words in the box into two sets.

baby	cry	why	lady	reply	copy
lorry	supply	tiny	multiply	rely	sunny

Words in which the **y** sounds like **ee**.

Words in which the **y** sounds like **ie**.

Challenge 3 Choose the correct word to match the picture.

a can/cane **b** kit/kite **c** rob/robe **d** plum/plume

Challenge 4 Change the **r** in **rate** to:

a d *date*   **b** f _____   **c** g _____

d l _____   **e** pl _____

Challenge 5 Make some words. Add either **oat** or **ound** to complete each word.

a c _____   **b** f _____   **c** g _____

d s _____   **e** thr _____

f p _____   **g** fl _____   **h** r _____

Challenge 6 Choose **wh** or **ph** to complete each word.

a __ __ at   **f** gra __ __

b ne __ __ ew   **g** __ __ isper

c __ __ ere   **h** trium __ __

d __ __ eel   **i** or __ __ an

e al __ __ abet   **j** __ __ imper

Allakazan! You have successfully completed the last activity, my apprentice! You have earned the last gold star for your certificate.

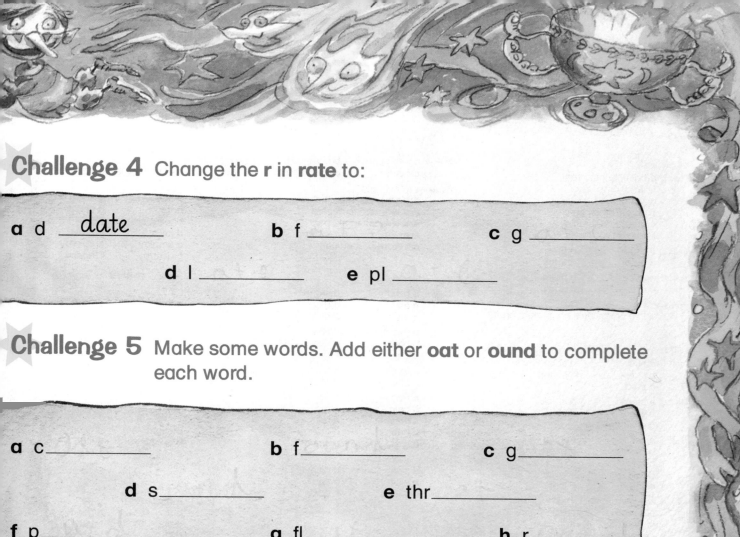

29

Answers

Pages 2–3

Task 1 **a** brick, bring, brag
b drag, drop, drip
c pram, prod, prop
d crack, crust, crop
e grab, grip, gruff
f trap, truck, trip

Task 2 **a** drum   **b** grass
c pram   **d** truck

Task 3 **a** truck   **b** pram
c drum   **d** grass

Sorcerer's Skill Check
brick, brag, crick, crag, drag, gruff

Pages 4–5

Task 1 **a** stick   **d** sting
b stack   **e** stamp
c stop

Task 2 **a** stamp   **d** stack
b sting   **e** stop
c stick

Task 3 **a** fist   **f** must
b best   **g** past
c fast   **h** dust
d rest   **i** cost
e list   **j** lost

Task 4 **ast words:** fast, past
est words: best, rest
ist words: list, fist
ost words: cost, lost
ust words: must, dust

Sorcerer's Skill Check
st at beginning: stiff, stab, stand, stuck
st at end: test, rust, past, rest

Pages 6–7

Task 1 **a** peel   **g** pool
b feel   **h** cool
c heel   **i** fool
d peep   **j** boot
e keep   **k** root
f deep   **l** hoot

Task 2 **a** keep-deep   **d** week-peek
b room-zoom   **e** hoop-loop
c seed-weed   **f** hoof-roof

Task 3 **a** week   **f** troop
b free   **g** weep
c root   **h** green
d noon   **i** mood
e need   **j** heel

Sorcerer's Skill Check
a bee   **b** pool
c tree   **d** boot

Pages 8–9

Task 1 **a** bar   **b** far
c car   **d** jar

Task 2 **a** bark   **b** arch
c sharp   **d** scarf

Task 3 **a** bark   **d** part
b dark   **e** start
c shark   **f** chart

Task 4 **a** lark-spark   **b** barn-darn
c car-far   **d** march-starch

Sorcerer's Skill Check
arch words: march, starch
ard words: hard, card
ark words: mark, bark
arm words: farm, charm
art words: dart, part

Pages 10–11

Task 1 **a** bay   **d** say
b pay   **e** day
c hay   **f** may

Task 2 **a** tray   **d** clay
b hay   **e** play
c day   **f** stay

Task 3 **a** train   **b** paint
c pail   **d** afraid

Task 4 **a** rain   **f** fail
b pain   **g** mail
c stain   **h** rail
d brain   **i** nail
e grain   **j** snail

Sorcerer's Skill Check
a sway   **d** dismay
b wait   **e** spray
c faint   **f** chain

Pages 12–13

Task 1 **oy words (red):** a, d, e, g, i, k
oi words (blue): b, c, f, h, j, l

Task 2 **oy words:** boy, joy, toy, enjoy, annoy, destroy
oi words: boil, coin, hoist, choice, noise, foil

Task 3 **a** toy   **b** point
c coin   **d** destroy

Task 4 **a** enjoy   **b** boil
c point

Sorcerer's Skill Check
a spoil   **g** joy
b noisy   **h** annoy
c choice   **i** boy
d moist   **j** toy
e employ   **k** joint
f destroy   **l** avoid

Pages 14–15

Challenge 1
a brick, brand   **d** grab, gruff
b crash, crack   **e** pram, prod
c drip, drink   **f** trap, truck

Challenge 2
frost, just, wrist, mist, rest, lost, last, fast, dust, best

Challenge 3
a food   **e** week
b roof   **f** heel
c three   **g** moon
d pool   **h** bee

Challenge 4
a carpet   **d** market
b target   **e** sharpen
c darling   **f** harvest

Challenge 5
real words: a, c, d, e, f, h, l

Challenge 6
a boy   **g** voice
b toy   **h** choice
c toilet   **i** poison
d joy   **j** point
e employ   **k** convoy
f destroy   **l** annoy

Pages 16–17

Task 1 **a** high   **d** thigh
b sigh   **e** right
c nigh   **f** sight

Task 2 **a** high   **d** tight
b right   **e** sight
c light, bright   **f** night

Task 3, 4
sigh, high, frightened, light, night, right, sight, might, tight

Sorcerer's Skill Check
a might   **d** night
b bright   **e** sigh
c fright   **f** high

Page 18-19

Task 1 **a** baby   **g** try
b my   **h** handy
c tiny   **i** lady
d fly   **j** cry
e by   **k** copy
f body   **l** why

Task 2 **y sounds like ee:** baby, tiny, body, handy, lady, copy
y sounds like ie: my, fly, by, try, cry, why

Task 3 **a** rainy   **b** foggy
c snowy   **d** sunny

Task 4 **a** reply   **d** dry
b supply   **e** penny
c poppy   **f** funny

Sorcerer's Skill Check
y sounds like ee (red): lumpy, happy, tiny, risky, empty
y sounds like ie (blue): fry, multiply, apply, rely, shy

Pages 20–21

Task 1 **a** hate   **e** made
b cane   **f** ride
c pipe   **g** wine
d robe   **h** cute

Task 2 **a** tap   **e** mat
b cap   **f** hid
c pin   **g** shin
d rod   **h** mop

Task 3 **a** hat   **b** ride
c mop   **d** tube

Task 4 **a** I can ride my bike.
b I drink water from the tap.
c I can win the race.
d I hope you get well soon.

Sorcerer's Skill Check

a mile   d hope
b pane   e shine
c cube   f bare

Pages 22–23

Task 1   a cake   b lake
        c rake   d shake

Task 2   a came   b same
        c blame   d shame

Task 3   a pile-smile   c side-wide
        b wise-rise   d hive-five

Task 4   a wide, side, hide
        b file, mile, smile
        c like, hike, bike
        d nine, fine, shine

Sorcerer's Skill Check

a tune   b prune
c tube   d mule

Pages 24–25

Task 1   boat-coat; soak-cloak; toad-road;
        coast-toast; moan-groan

Task 2   a about
        b cloud
        c sound
        d amount

Task 3   a toad   b cloud
        c mouse   d mouth

Task 4   a fountain
        b toadstool
        c toast

Sorcerer's Skill Check

Many answers are possible.

Pages 26–27

Task 1   a when   f phone
        b where   g graph
        c why   h dolphin
        d who   I photo
        e which   j alphabet

Task 2   a who or why
        b when
        c phone or graph or photo
        d dolphin

Task 3   a whiskers   e elephant
        b telephone   f dolphin
        c whale   g wheat
        d wheel   h alphabet

Task 4   a telephone   b whale
        c wheat   d dolphin

Sorcerer's Skill Check

wh words: wheel, white, whisk,
whisper, wheat
ph words: phone, elephant,
dolphin, nephew, alphabet

Pages 28–29

Challenge 1

a high   f sigh
b thigh   g sight
c tight   h right
d might   I fight
e light   j bright

Challenge 2

y sounds like ee: baby, lady, copy,
lorry, tiny, sunny
y sounds like ie: cry, why, reply,
supply, multiply, rely

Challenge 3

a can   b kite
c robe   d plum

Challenge 4

a date   d late
b fate   e plate
c gate

Challenge 5

a coat   e throat
b found   f pound
c goat   g float
d sound   h round

Challenge 6

a what   f graph
b nephew   g whisper
c where   h triumph
d wheel   I orphan
e alphabet   j whimper

Wizard's Certificate of Excellence

Weird Word Beginnings

Incred igh

Wonderful st words

Fantastic y

Enchanted ee and oo

Introducing the Magic e

Astonishing ar

Advanced Magic with e

Amazing ay and ai

Using ou and oa

Obliging oi and oy

Wacky wh and ph

Apprentice Wizard Challenge 1

Apprentice Wizard Challenge 2

This is to state that Wizard Whimstaff awards

Apprentice _____

the title of English Wizard. Congratulations!

Published 2002
Revised edition 2007

01/091210

Published by Letts Educational Ltd.
An imprint of HarperCollins*Publishers*
77–85 Fulham Palace Road
London W6 8JB

Text © Louis Fidge
Design and illustrations © 2002 Letts Educational Ltd.

Author: Louis Fidge
Book Concept and Development:
Helen Jacobs; Sophie London
Design and Editorial: 2idesign, Cambridge
Cover Design: Linda Males
Illustrations: Mike Phillips and Neil Chapman (Beehive illustration)
Cover Illustration: Neil Chapman

British Library Cataloguing in Publication Data

A CIP record for this book is available from the British Library.

ISBN 978 1 84315 109 8

Printed in the UK